NOTES

by
J. L. Roberts, Ph.D.
Professor of English
University of Nebraska

Cliffs Notes
INCORPORATED
LINCOLN, NEBRASKA 68501

Editor

Gary Carey, M.A.
University of Colorado

Consulting Editor

James L. Roberts, Ph.D.
Department of English
University of Nebraska

Cliffs Notes, Inc.   Lincoln, Nebraska

CONTENTS

SHANE
Notes

LIFE OF THE AUTHOR

It is most unusual that Jack Schaefer, best known for his western novels, did not encounter the West until many of his western novels had achieved widespread fame. In fact, at the time of his writing *Shane,* Schaefer had never been farther west than Toledo, Ohio. He was born in Cleveland, Ohio, in 1907 to an upper middle-class family. His father, Carl, was a competent lawyer and also a history buff, as well as an enthusiastic collector of Lincoln memorabilia, which was probably one of the reasons for his friendship with Carl Sandburg, who later wrote extensively about Lincoln.

Early in his life, Jack Schaefer was attracted to the written word. In high school, he edited the school literary magazine, and at Oberlin College, he took courses in creative writing along with an emphasis on the classical Greek and Roman masterpieces of literature.

In 1929, Schaefer entered Columbia University for graduate study in English. Very early, it was clear that he was not happy with the restricted view of graduate study at that time. Whereas in more recent times, the study of motion pictures has come to be accepted as a highly respected field of study, when Schaefer proposed a thesis on the development of themes in motion pictures, he was ridiculed by the conservative faculty, which looked upon movies as cheap escapism. As a result of this experience, Schaefer apparently developed a hostility against almost everything that was associated with academia and particularly with graduate study. He has stated that graduate schools encourage graduate students to impose meanings on literary works that were never intended by the original author. He also resents literary quarterlies because they are snobbish and encourage "silly jargon and critical gobbledygook."

After leaving college, Schaefer worked briefly in the educational field (as assistant director of education at the Connecticut State Reformatory), but his main interest at the time was journalism. After having worked on newspapers in New Haven and Baltimore, he became one of the editorial writers for the *Norfolk Virginian—Pilot*. It was during this period of his life that he read extensively about the history of the West and also wrote *Shane*. In fact, Schaefer's experience in writing editorials is reflected in his creative writing. His style is almost journalistic in the sense that it is unadorned and uncomplicated. His style is direct, simple, and clear. He is able, as he was in his editorials, to express his ideas with clarity and forcefulness and simplicity. For example, look at the directness, the simplicity, and crispness of the opening sentence of *Shane:* "He rode into our valley in the summer of '89." This one simple sentence captures the essence of the novel.

Schaefer is also interested in telling a good story. He writes that he "thinks and writes in the direct, old-fashioned manner and likes to believe that he is bumbling along in the ancient tradition of the tale-tellers." This view could be, in part, the result of his studies in Greek literature, where the emphasis was on the plot or the narrative, as in the *Iliad* and the *Odyssey*.

After *Shane* was completed in 1946, Schaefer submitted it to *Argosy* magazine, which published it as a three-part serial under the title of "Rider from Nowhere." In 1949, Houghton Mifflin published *Shane* in book form, and in 1954, an illustrated edition was brought out which deleted nineteen uses of the words "hell" and "damn" because it was believed that these words might be offensive to the parents of young readers.

In 1953, *Shane* was made into a movie which was extremely popular. The reviews were, all in all, very favorable, and as a result, the novel also gained a wider audience. Since *Shane,*

Schaefer has taken up residence in New Mexico and has produced a number of other novels and numerous short stories about the West. Of his novels other than *Shane,* the most popular and critically accepted are *The Canyon* (1953), which is, like *Shane,* another novel about growing up and about self-realization; *Monte Walsh* (1963), a long historical novel about the life of a cowboy; and *Mavericks* (1967), another tale about early cowboy days. But ultimately, *Shane* will probably remain Schaefer's best known novel.

BASIC THEMES IN *SHANE*

Jack Schaefer's *Shane* is a guidepost by which many western novels are judged, and since its publication in 1949, it has become a classic in the literature of the American West. This is unusual because an author's first novel, as *Shane* was Schaefer's first novel, does not often receive such high acclaim.

Another unusual aspect of this novel is that it was written by a man who had never been west of Ohio at the time he wrote the novel. Furthermore, according to Schaefer's own account, he had never even read any "western novels"; in fact, in an interview with Henry J. Nuwer (see *South Dakota Review* 11, Spring, 1973), Schaefer maintained: "I was not reading western stories then. I read history. I only read a few of the better westerns. In fact, if I had known of the tremendous amount of bad western writing that was flooding the market I wouldn't have written anything."

Thus, in one way, *Shane* can be looked upon as a historical novel about the West because Schaefer's first interest was in history. Schaefer says that during the writing of *Shane,* he worked at two jobs "sixteen hours a day! Anyway when I was through working, I read books on American history." He was particularly interested in the history of the American West, and he also maintained that his early education was extremely valuable in providing him with the ability to do full-time research into a historical field such as the American West. Schaefer's knowledge of the historical times gives this novel a ring of authenticity; it reads as though he lived in this Wyoming district during the time of its settlement.

The fact that *Shane* has had and continues to have a broad audience – from mainstream readers to historians to literary critics and finally to the movie industry and the moviegoers – suggests that *Shane* can be read on many levels and that it speaks to the reader concerning complex social themes as well as accurate, historical ideas.

The primary reading of the novel is the age-old conflict between the homesteader and the rancher, or between the pioneer farmer and the cattle baron who needs the open range. More romantically, the conflict is between those who want to fence in the range and bring civilization (law and order, schools, and churches) to bear upon the area and those who want to keep an open range and live by the law of the land (sometimes called "the law of two guns"). Many variations upon these basic themes can be found. For example, the basic literary technique here is simple: the introduction of a foreign element into an otherwise stable or established way of life. A variation often seen in many western novels and movies is the encounter or conflict arising when the sheepherder arrives and intrudes upon the cattle baron; this age-old conflict between those who raise sheep and those who raise cattle illustrates the introduction of a new, and sometimes destructive, element into a prosperous community.

Shane can also be profitably read as an excellent example of the initiation or the maturation story – or stated in its most simple terms, the theme of growing up – a theme that Schaefer uses in many of his works. The story here is told from the viewpoint of Bob Starrett, an adult looking back on his childhood, recalling for us the tremendous influence that a stranger, Shane, had on his life while Bob was growing up. In other words, Shane's presence became an incredible and enduring moment in a boy's childhood – an event so enormous and so memorable as to never be forgotten, a lesson learned that will remain with

Bob Starrett forever. Shane has touched this boy in an unforgettable manner – both by his own example and by his individual lessons.

Other and more complicated historical readings of the novel are possible. For example, we can see the essential conflict as being between two or three types of historical waves of settlements. The first wave was that of the pioneers who depended on the open range, unrestricted freedom, and on virtually no agriculture. This was followed by subsequent waves of settlers who were more interested in establishing permanency, cultivating the land, and building structures meant to last. A final wave were those people who came to the West with money and enterprise in order to develop the land for profit and civilization. Clearly, *Shane* can be read as an example of the historical settlements of the West and the various difficulties encountered when one wave, represented by Fletcher, is unfortunately followed too quickly by a subsequent wave, represented by Joe and Marian Starrett.

Likewise, *Shane* is also filled with a surprising number of literary analogues, or analogies, and references to classical myths. These allusions are not important to a basic reading of the novel, but they add depth and richness to the novel for the mature reader. Perhaps this final idea is best represented by the symbolic meaning of the stump on the Starrett farm. It extends deeper into the ground than anyone can see, and the deeper meanings of *Shane* also extend far beneath the surface or obvious meanings of the novel. *Shane*, therefore, appeals to the reader on levels that the reader is not always aware of.

Shane can also be read and valued as an example of the archetype of the western novel. Stated in other terms, this novel possesses the archetypal patterns that are now the criteria by which other western novels are measured. By the term "archetypal," we mean the original pattern or model after which something is made. In other words, the general outline of *Shane* is the pattern, or idea, or formula that is found in countless numbers of western novels.

Observe the pattern: (1) An unknown stranger comes (2) out of nowhere and (3) possesses no background and no allegiances. (4) He is a person of mystery and evokes various responses – good responses from the good people like the Starretts and fearful responses from people like Fletcher and Wilson. (5) The stranger arrives at a moment of major crisis even though (6) he is not aware of the impending crisis. (7) Before the crisis, there is often (but not always) a minor demonstration – such as the removal of the stump – which foreshadows his climactic success later on. (8) The character is confronted with the crisis which usually climaxes in terms of (9) a barroom brawl (usually set against a background of poker chips, swinging doors, and whiskey), and later, (10) a shootout, often with a hired killer. (11) After the shootout, the stranger rides away, never to be heard of again, but (12) he has made a tremendous impact on the community and on some of the individual members of the community. *Shane* contains a perfect example of this classical pattern, and variations of this pattern can be found in numerous other westerns.

LIST OF CHARACTERS

Shane

The main character of the novel; he has only this single name. In the classic sense, Shane appears from out of nowhere, performs unbelievable feats of skill and courage, creates a lasting impression on the people, and then rides off into the distance, never to be heard of again.

THE HOMESTEADERS

Joe Starrett

The homesteader who hires Shane. Joe is a powerfully built man, physically larger than Shane yet not possessing that illusive power that Shane has. Joe is a good and brave man who is looked upon as the leader and spokesman for the homesteaders.

Marian Starrett

Joe's wife, who is competent and intelligent. She is exceptionally proud of her cooking, which becomes a symbol of the beginning of civilization in the West.

Bob Starrett

Bob is the narrator of the story; he is the first one in the valley to see Shane, and he is the one who will be the most influenced by Shane. By the end of the story, Shane will have touched the boy so profoundly that as an adult man, Bob will narrate this story about his first encounter with Shane.

Young Morley

A young hired man who works for Joe Starrett until some of Fletcher's men beat him up. He comes back to the Starrett farm bruised and beaten, gathers up his possessions, curses Joe for hiring him, and rides away. This young hired man is introduced as a contrast to Shane. Whereas Fletcher's men are able to frighten young Morley off, Shane will not be intimidated by Fletcher or by his men.

Henry Shipstead

One of the original homesteaders; his farm is closest to town. He is a good farmer who comes from Iowa.

Lew Johnson

Another of the original homesteaders who, along with Henry Shipstead, represents solid, dependable men – the old line of farmers who made the West their permanent home.

Ollie Johnson

Lew Johnson's son; he is Bob Starrett's friend, even though Bob can beat him in a fight. The two boys play hookey and go fishing together.

James Lewis and Ed Howells

Two homesteaders who tagged along when they found out that Joe Starrett was going to homestead in this area. They do not have Joe's energy, drive, or incentive, and they could easily be driven off their property if it were not for people like Joe Starrett, who holds them all together.

Frank Torrey

Another homesteader; he lives farther up the valley. He is a nervous and fidgety type and cannot be trusted in an emergency. He has a griping, complaining wife and "a string of dirty kids growing longer every year." Torrey's stubborn streak makes him want to defy Fletcher.

Ernie Wright

Another homesteader; he is large, husky, and likable, but he is a weak man who loves singing and telling tall stories. He would rather be out hunting than working. His quick temper leads him into the trap that Fletcher sets for him, and it costs him his life.

THE CATTLE RANCHERS

Luke Fletcher

A large landowner and cattle rancher who needs a large range for his cattle. The homesteaders have begun fencing off portions of the range that Fletcher believes he needs for his cattle. Therefore, he becomes the single most powerful force which opposes the homesteaders. Physically, Fletcher is a tall man who might have been handsome at one time. He wears only fine clothes, which emphasize his arrogance and his reckless determination. The crisis between Fletcher and the homesteaders occurs when Fletcher receives a large contract to supply beef to the Indian Agent for the Sioux reservation. As a rancher in need of open range, he is unprincipled in his methods, and, not surprisingly, he hires a gunfighter to get into arguments with the homesteaders so as to have a motive for killing them. In the climactic scene between Shane and the gunfighter, Fletcher is on the balcony of the saloon and tries to shoot Shane in the back. This act puts an effective end to Fletcher's tyranny over the valley. Afterward, every man is against him, even the mild Mr. Weir.

Morgan

He is Fletcher's overseer, a dedicated cattleman who hates homesteaders with a passion. He is big and heavy-set, with a powerful build – "a broad slab of a man with flattened face and head small in proportion to great sloping shoulders." One might think that he could easily annihilate someone of Shane's stature because Morgan physically towers above Shane and because Morgan uses any kind of underhanded, dirty tactics in order to win. In spite of Morgan's tremendous, hulking size, however, on a one-to-one basis, Morgan is no match for the more agile and skillful Shane.

Chris

He is a young cowboy working for Fletcher. He is known for his lighthearted manner and for his reckless courage. Even though Chris is not given a last name, he represents the type of person who can be completely changed by Shane. On his first encounter with Shane, he deliberately shouts insults about Shane and about "dirt farmers" who raise pigs. Exercising great restraint, Shane ignores Chris and leaves the saloon. However, Chris, in his youthful enthusiasm, cannot let the story drop, and he begins spreading the word that the homesteaders are really pig farmers. The story is told so often that all the homesteaders have difficulty holding up their heads in town because of all the teasing. Finally, Shane has to confront young Chris even though he doesn't want to. In the fight, Chris is beaten and his arm is broken. However, Chris learns later that in spite of his youthful recklessness, Shane still considers him the only man among Fletcher's bullies who is worth redeeming. The proof of this comes at the end of the novel when Chris comes to Joe Starrett and asks for Shane's job, acknowledging, though, that he will never be as good a man as Shane. Thus, young Chris has been redeemed by Shane and by Shane's examples.

Red Marlin

Another of Fletcher's cowboys. He sits in the background and enjoys young Chris' insulting remarks about the homesteaders, but when it comes to a confrontation with Shane, he wisely (or cowardly) slinks away. After the fight between Chris and Shane, Red Marlin "sat quiet like he was trying not even to breathe." He is a frightened man, and he doesn't care if other people know it. The others, having seen what Shane did to Chris, don't blame him for being frightened.

Curly

Another of Fletcher's cowhands. Because of his lumbering size ("he was thick and powerful"), Morgan brings him to help beat up Shane, but in spite of his size, Curly (so named because of his "shock of unruly hair") is stupid and slow-moving.

THE GUNSHOOTER

Stark Wilson

His first name – "Stark" – implies something about the starkness associated with him. In general, though, Wilson represents the outside, evil force which is brought into the valley to wreak havoc and destruction in order to bring a full measure of injustice, fear, and terror to the unsettled land. He is the "law of the West," or the "law of two guns." It is, therefore, fitting that as a gunslinger, he carries two guns and is known to be just as good on the draw with one hand as he is with the other. Reportedly, he is as fast on the draw as the best of them. He is dressed in typical gunslinger clothes—that is, he wears matching pants and coat, with his two guns pegged down at the tips with thin straps fastened around his thighs. He is tall, and he walks with a swagger. His eyes are cold and mean. When Wilson and Fletcher come to Joe Starrett's place, Wilson is "sure of himself, serene and deadly." But when it comes to encountering Shane in the saloon, Wilson's "face sobered and his eyes glinted coldly." Wilson does not want to get in a quarrel with Shane because he knows that he has met a man as cool and as deadly as he is. Yet Wilson, true to his vocation as a killer, does not back down: he meets Shane and is killed by him.

THE TOWNSPEOPLE

Mr. Grafton

The owner of the general store and the adjoining saloon, which make up the main building in town. He represents the earliest efforts toward civilization, and while he does not approve of fights in his saloon, he does not interfere.

Jane Grafton

His daughter; she is the school teacher, and as such, she also represents the beginnings of civilization for the frontier.

Will Atkey

Mr. Grafton's thin, "sad-faced clerk and bartender."

Mr. Weir

A friendly townsman who keeps the stage post. He is

responsible for making Ernie Wright's coffin, and after the shoot-out, he takes Bob Starrett back to the farm. He represents the attitude of the town, which is slowly turning against Fletcher's high-handed supremacy.

Ledyard

The traveling peddler or trader who brings a cultivator to Joe Starrett's; when he tries to overcharge Joe, Shane points out that he saw the same cultivator in Cheyenne for fifty dollars less. The fact that Joe takes Shane's word for it indicates how quickly Joe has come to trust Shane.

CRITICAL COMMENTARIES

Chapter 1

The opening chapter centers on Shane, the main character, whom we will constantly see through the eyes of the young narrator. Essentially, young Bob Starrett is narrating the story, and ultimately, Shane will have the most influence upon Bob and will create in Bob such a lasting and deep impression that Bob, in adult life, will return to his memories of Shane's arrival in the valley and will tell his entire story. As the first part of the story is told from a future distance in time, so our first glimpse of Shane is from a distance.

This first view of Shane is as though he is just another cow-hand ("another stray horseman") riding past, but then both Bob and the reader are alerted to something "different" about him when two other cowhands "stop and stare after him with a curious intentness."

As Bob is sitting on the fence rail watching Shane, he sees him hesitate at a fork in the road: one road leads to Luke Fletcher's big cattle ranch and the other road leads to the land occupied by the homesteaders. Thus, in the third paragraph of the novel, Schaefer has already introduced his basic theme — the two ways of life represented in the valley: the cattle rancher versus the homesteaders. The implied conflict is told in its simplest journalistic terms, leaving nothing to supposition.

If one is familiar with the customs of the West of that day, then the description of Shane's clothing takes on significance. Since he wears a pair of serge trousers with a matching coat and a finespun linen shirt and wears an unusual felt hat, we know this is not the outfit of a typical cowhand; instead, it is the outfit traditionally worn by a professional gambler or gunslinger. Except for the absence of the guns, it is almost exactly like the outfit that Stark Wilson will wear when he comes to town to kill off the homesteaders. Thus, even though we are never to know anything about Shane's real past, we are given here, and elsewhere, enough information to know that he is not an average cowhand.

In looking at Shane and in remembering him from a distance in time, Bob Starrett lets us know that Shane was *not* a big man—it was, instead, the things that Shane did which made him *seem* big. Actually, Shane is rather "slight" in build, and next to Joe Starrett, he could seem to be frail, but there is a strength and an endurance in him which Bob had never seen in another person. Bob writes that he "could read the endurance in the lines of that dark figure and the quiet power in its effortless, unthinking adjustment to every movement of the tired horse." These obviously are not the observations of the young Bob Starrett, but those of the older Bob, who has had time to reflect upon Shane's qualities.

As Shane is approaching the farmhouse, Bob gives us a description of the farm. It is a place where there are garden plots for vegetables, a field of potatoes, and a field of a new variety of corn for the livestock. More rare than anything else in this part of the country is the house—painted white with green trim. At this time in the West, a painted house was an almost unheard-of thing. Thus, we see immediately that the Starretts are attempting to bring touches of civilization to this wild, untamed land. This desire for civilization is also symbolized in Marian's cooking, which is far better than the ordinary food one would get as a farmhand. Marian is very proud of her cooking, feeling that it is one part of New England civilization that she has brought with her to the frontier. This emphasis upon civilization will be part of the conflict between the homesteaders and the rancher: the homesteaders represent the need and desire for civilization in terms of fenced-in lands – representing a sense of permanency – as opposed to the open spaces and open laws of the large ranches.

Joe Starrett and Shane meet over the sharing of water, a communal ritual that goes back to biblical and classical Greek times. Already as young Bob watches Shane, he sees a kind of magnificence emerge as Shane shows "the strength of quality and competence." Later, when young Bob is helping Shane with his horse, and Shane compliments the boy, this creates a deep glow in the boy; he has been praised by his new hero. Shane immediately becomes a role model, and ultimately an idol for the young, impressionable boy. But the young boy does not recognize this; it is, instead, the grown man who is narrating the story who knows this. For example, often the adult narrator will let the readers know that there were things passed between the adults that he, as a boy, did not understand: "I stared in wonder as father and the stranger looked at each other . . . in an unspoken fraternity of adult knowledge beyond my reach."

Perhaps nothing characterizes Shane so much as does his name. After Joe Starrett has introduced himself and his son, the stranger says simply, "Call me Shane." Certainly, Schaefer was aware that America's great literary masterpiece, *Moby Dick*, begins with the simple sentence "Call me Ishmael." The use of only one name adds mystery and universality to Shane. Many great, popular men have gone by one simple name which sets them apart from other people. Shane is one of those people.

At supper that evening, both Joe and Marian try to find out more about Shane, but he recognizes their purpose and is able to put them off without revealing anything about himself. And by the end of the novel, we will know no more about Shane than we do now. "His past was fenced as tightly as our pasture."

Likewise at supper that night, Joe, in explaining his aims and methods for running his farm, also characterizes the nature of the conflict between the farmers and the cattle barons. To Joe, cattle ranching has proved to be wasteful. He has been able to raise cattle that are 300 pounds heavier than the cattle which Fletcher drives to the stockyards. Also, Joe mentions casually that the ranchers, the cattle barons, find the farmers a nuisance because they have cut up the range and, in some cases, have blocked part of the water supply. Thus, a conflict will burst out later when Fletcher thinks that he needs all of the range for his cattle ranching.

The first chapter ends with Joe and Marian discussing Shane's gentleness and the fact that despite his sense of gentleness, there is something mysterious and dangerous about him. This first chapter, narrated with such simplicity, presents to the reader a wealth of information about the characters and the themes to be investigated.

Chapter 2

After the basic introduction of the characters in Chapter 1, this chapter shows Shane complimenting Marian's superb cooking. Then Shane promises to stay for the day since it is raining and also because Marian promises to make a deep-dish apple pie. Shane describes the newest ladies' fashions "back in civilization," and later Joe proudly shows Shane around the farm, and in particular, he shows him the stump on his land. Then Schaefer describes the significant encounter between Shane and Ledyard, the peddler, and the chapter ends as Joe and Shane return to attack the stump until it is time for Marian's supper.

The opening of the chapter seems insignificant with the discussion about Marian's "flapjacks," which Shane complimentarily refers to by the more elegant name of "flannel cakes," a name that suggests refinement and culture. The emphasis on Marian's food is to remind the reader of her attempt to bring civilization to the frontier. One of the lesser reasons for Shane's later remaining on the farm is that Marian's cooking is so outstanding.

Throughout the remainder of the novel, there will be slight, and we emphasize slight, or minor, sexual overtones (or more accurately, undertones) between Marian and Shane. This basic sexual attraction is first hinted at when Marian giggles like a girl at Shane's compliments. Her attraction is further suggested in her anxiousness and in her enthusiastic support of his becoming the new hired hand. However, the sexual attraction is completely underplayed until the appearance of Wilson – when Wilson's guarded insult brings it out in the open.

We should remember that for Bob, the young boy-narrator, the talk about women's hats and general fashion styles seems "foolish to be coming from a grown man." Yet Shane, the mature adult, is comfortable with the subject. It is important to note here that the talk once again emphasizes the differences between civilized society and the society here on the frontier, and the fact that Marian, in these small ways, is trying to bring even the smallest aspects of civilization to the frontier.

Later, Joe is delighted to show off the farm to Shane, and even though Shane is reserved and reticent about his own background, he is able to bring out Joe's natural talkativeness. While showing Shane about the farm, Joe suddenly notices that Shane is not paying attention. Instead, his eyes are riveted upon a gigantic stump: "It stuck out like an old scarred sore – a big old stump all jagged across the top." The "huge old roots" are sent out in all directions and are twisting deeply into the ground, well below the surface. This stump will be the main subject of the next chapter.

The stump is imbued with various types of meaning – it is an image of strength and firmness and solidarity: it is also the metaphor or the symbol of the unchanging frontier which does not want to yield to civilization. For Joe, it is an "old scarred sore" and "the millstone round my neck" which becomes his personal battle with the frontier and resists Joe's civilizing efforts. The stump is the "one fool thing about this place I haven't licked yet." And since he has been unable to "lick" it himself, we feel certain that Shane will be able to do so.

The stump is also symbolic of the challenge which the frontier holds for all pioneers, and it is a symbol of the task that must be completed before man's right to the land is complete. The depth of the roots suggests that much of the stump's meaning lies beneath the surface in the same way that much of Shane's power as a man lies beneath his gentle, surface appearance. The roots are the unseen power of the thing—just as Shane's or Joe's strengths are also largely beneath the surface.

The stump has also been used for Joe to vent his anger on, and yet the stump remains and seems to "jeer" at Joe. Nothing works against it until Shane comes along and attacks it himself, and as we see in the next chapter, Shane is finally able to help Joe remove the stump. Note also that Joe makes a vague correlation between the stump and Shane when he says that the stump is tough and that he can admire toughness—a quality that Joe has already recognized in Shane.

The arrival of Ledyard, the peddler, provides the readers with another chance to evaluate Shane. Ledyard is disliked by Bob, our narrator, and thus, the reader's view is colored by Bob's dislike. Note, however, that when Ledyard tries to overcharge Joe for the new, seven-pronged cultivator, Shane immediately comments that he saw one for about half that price in Cheyenne. Ledyard tries to cast spurious remarks about Shane's reputation, referring to him as a "cheap tinhorn" and a "tramp"—but suddenly, Ledyard catches a view of Shane and "fell back a step with a sudden fear." Our narrator, Bob, also notices Shane's changed appearance. In addition, there is a chill in the air that is intangible and terrifying. And yet Shane is simply standing there with his hands clenched. However, there is a sense that any second could "bring a burst of indescribable deadliness." This is the same type of deeply embedded fear and abject terror that Mr. Grafton later sees in Shane when Shane first refuses to fight Chris: that is, Shane's face in the later barroom encounter with Chris will be filled with fear—but not fear of Chris. Instead, Shane is afraid that he cannot control his own anger.

When Ledyard throws down the challenge—"Are you going to take his [Shane's] word over mine?"—it is easy for Joe to answer: "I can figure men for myself. I'll take his word on anything he wants to say any day of God's whole year." Thus, even though Joe has apparently known Ledyard for years, and although he has known Shane for only about twelve hours, Shane has already inspired a trust and a confidence in a good man like Starrett, and in contrast, he has caused fear and intangible terror in a weak man like Ledyard.

After Joe's statement of confidence in Shane, Shane responds to the compliment in about the only manner he can. He gets an axe and begins to attack Joe's nemesis (his troubling or avenging enemy), the stump. Watching him, Bob sees Shane as his ideal—the perfect role model: "He was a man like father in whom a boy could believe in the simple knowing that what was beyond comprehension was still clean and solid and right." These are not the words and language of a young boy; these sentiments are the expression of an adult man looking back on his youth and realizing that even though he could not always understand what Shane did, yet whatever this man did, it had to be "clean and solid and right" simply because Shane did it.

When Shane explains that he is chopping away at the stump because "a man has to pay his debts," Bob thinks that Shane is trying to pay for his supper and breakfast, but Joe tells Bob that Shane didn't mean meals; rather, Shane wants to repay Joe for the trust that Joe expressed in him.

As Bob watches Shane chopping at the roots of the stump, he sees in Shane the perfect image of the real man of strength and will, pitted against an unmoveable object. Shane seems poised and at one with the axe. Then, when Joe comes out with the other axe, together the two men form a union, a comradeship grown out of mutual trust and mutual respect: "Their eyes met over the top of the stump and held and neither one of them said a word. Then they swung up their axes and both of them said plenty to that old stump." It is an inspiration and a lesson to the boy about manly relations. This chapter, then, focuses on the making of a hero and the origins of a legendary figure, the myth of Shane.

Chapter 3

This chapter is devoted almost entirely to the battle with the great stump; however, Schaefer gives almost as much attention to Marian's own "battle" to bring civilization to the frontier.

As Shane and Joe are chopping away at the stump, Marian interrupts them to ask Shane his opinion about her newly refurbished old hat, and throughout the chapter Marian continues to interrupt the men—offering advice about using a team of horses to finish pulling out the stump, sending out freshly baked biscuits, watching them through a peekhole in the barn, and finally making a second deep-dish apple pie for them. Marian's constant presence and particularly her wearing the newly altered hat, trying to look like the fashionable ladies whom Shane described, suggests her infatuation with Shane. Caught up by the presence of Shane, she has changed. She wants to compete with the fashionable, "civilized" ladies for Shane's attention.

Clearly, however, the central episode is the battle, or the struggle, with the gigantic stump which, as noted in the discussion of the last chapter, becomes a central, symbolic image in the novel. It is not necessary to attach a single, specific or definite symbolic meaning to it, but all of the meanings suggested in the last discussion will apply. Even the men are only vaguely aware of the meaning inherent in the stump: "Their minds were on that old stump and whatever it was that old stump had come to mean to them." When Marian asks Bob what went on out there, wondering, "What got into those two?", she is vaguely aware of something mysterious which binds the two men together and which excludes her. We will discover that the success with the stump foreshadows Shane's success with

Chris, with the gang fight, and ultimately his victory over the gunslinging killer, Wilson.

Joe and Shane work all afternoon on the massive stump, never speaking to each other except through their glances. Young Bob cannot understand, "could not grasp how they could stick at it hour after hour" because "that old stump was not really so important." Interestingly, the stump is of great importance to the men. It is the great challenge that they must face and overcome. To the boy, at that time, the stump was not important, but in his adult life, when he comes back to narrate the event, he then sees and communicates to the reader the extreme significance of the stump, because as noted in the above paragraph, the success in this first challenge will lead directly to the success of other challenges.

Symbol of Stump

Likewise, Marian doesn't understand the nature of the challenge when she suggests, "Why don't you . . . hitch up the team? Horses will have it out in no time at all." She cannot understand that it is the struggle itself that is important – *not* just the mere fact of ridding the land of any old stump – and that the men themselves must complete the task that they themselves began.

Late in the afternoon, Shane and Joe discover that the stump is bound to the earth by a deeply embedded tap root which is virtually inaccessible. Therefore, Joe uses his great hulking weight to pull up the stump so that the more sprightly Shane can stoop over and begin cutting away at the tap root. Alone, neither man would be able to perform the task – Shane is too slight to push the massive stump forward, and Joe has too much bulk to be agile enough to get to the tap root. But working together, the two men can perform a task and can conquer a challenge that would elude either of them separately.

Together, the two men defeat the massive stump and all that it stands for. Throughout the struggle and especially when the stump is "defeated," the stump itself takes on almost human qualities as though it were "an old friend." And the final image of the defeated stump will remain vivid in the boy's memory until he becomes the man who will remember the moment: "This was one of the things you would never forget whatever time might do to you in the furrowing of the years, an old stump on its side with root ends making a strange pattern against the glow of the sun sinking behind the far mountains and two men looking over it into each other's eyes." With its removal, Joe Starrett says to <u>Marian: "I'm rested now,"</u> meaning that his inner self <u>is now at peace since the stump is gone.</u> #6B

In the midst of the struggle with the stump, seemingly the last physical obstacle between Starrett and his conquering the frontier, Marian sends out a plate of biscuits. The ordinary farm wife would probably have sent out something cool to drink, but since Marian prides herself on her cooking, and since cooking is a key symbol of civilization for her, she sends only the delicate biscuits. Joe is careful to divide them equally, thus acknowledging Shane to be fully his equal. It is as though in sharing the biscuits, there is a type of religious communion between them.

Then as Marian watches "in wide-eyed wonder," she forgets about her apple pie and it burns. However, her irritation and determination to make a second pie can be explained by these considerations: (1) the men won their fight against the stump and Marian failed to make a promised pie (their victory and her defeat). In addition, Marian was (2) so fascinated by the brute force and muscular strength of the two physically powerful and attractive men that (3) she forgot one of the symbols of her civilized society, and (4) the second pie had to be made in order for her to acknowledge the power of civilization over the raw, brute forces of the frontier.

It is also important to note that just as this chapter began with the ominous, threatening presence of the stump, it ends with the <u>conquest of the stump and the success</u> of the apple pie. There is laughter all around the table; the Starretts and Shane are enjoying the simple pleasures of life.

Chapter 4

Essentially, this chapter fills in many details about Shane — particularly about his physical stature and about the effect he has on Bob's mother and father. We are also given many conjectural opinions about him.

Shane's influence on young Bob is immediately evident when Bob, waking next morning, charges out of his room fearing that Shane might have left without saying goodbye. Instead, he finds Shane and Joe discussing the nature of farming in ranching country. Shane hears about Fletcher, the cattle baron who is trying to crowd Joe and the other homesteaders out. Joe explains to Shane that his last hired hand left after he was roughed up by some of Fletcher's men, and then Joe offers Shane a job as the Starretts' hired hand. Shane accepts, but he asserts that he never planned on becoming a farmer.

Later, Bob is surprised at how well Shane takes to the job, and he is perplexed when Shane deliberately takes his father's chair at the dinner table until he realizes later that Shane does not like to sit with his back to the door. Bob's views of Shane become more complex when he discovers a magnificent gun in Shane's saddle-roll, for Shane, unlike other men, never wears his gun.

At the beginning of the chapter, the young narrator's first thoughts are on Shane, and while it is true that any stranger or guest would be a welcome change to the long monotony of the frontier, Shane is much more than just any chance visitor. From a distant perspective in time, Bob is able to look back, and while he "could not straighten out in my mind the way the grown folks had behaved," yet now as an adult, he can present these significant discussions.

While thinking about Shane, Bob remembers how different the man seemed as a hired man than when he had first appeared, "chilling in his dark solitude, riding up our road." Bob realizes that part of Shane's greatness was the effect that he had on his father. The effect was definite but vague — "something not of words or of actions but of the essential substance of the human spirit." Bob, first as a boy and then as the older narrator, is constantly reminded of how Shane brought about a change in both Bob's father and mother: "They were more alive and more vibrant." And even if Shane did come out of a "closed and guarded" past, the influence upon the Starrett family is definitely a good influence.

Before Joe Starrett offers Shane a job, he asks Shane straight-forwardly if he is running away from something. Shane responds ambiguously: he is not running away from anything—"not in the way you mean." The implication, however, is that he is run-ning away from something, and we can only speculate as to what that "something" is. Essentially, the sensitive reader would assume that Shane is trying to escape from his past, from a shooting or a killing that he performed against his will. This view would help explain his reluctance to get into a fight and his own personal conflict when he has to meet Wilson, the gun-slinging killer. At that time, we will see that Shane does not relish killing, but when he has to confront Wilson, killing seems to be forced upon him as part of his life.

When Joe offers Shane the job as hired hand, he does not gloss over matters. He makes it clear that his principal aim is farming—not ranching. As he tells Shane, "I've got a job to do here," and what he means, at least subconsciously, is that he wants to do more than farm. He wants to establish civilization— that is, the farm itself represents civilization. In contrast, Shane has never seriously considered working on a farm. In fact, as he later says, two days ago he would have scorned the idea; farming to a cowboy is a degrading step down. Yet here on the Starrett farm, with all of its human qualities, Shane feels com-fortably aligned. Furthermore, after hearing the story about how Joe's last hired hand (young Morley) was beaten up and fright-ened off by Luke Fletcher, Shane is fully aware that he, as the new hired hand, will be put under the same pressure and harass-ment, but he is willing to accept the challenge because of his attachment to the Starretts.

In a bit of perhaps too-obvious symbolism, before Shane

can begin work, he has to buy new clothes. New clothes will be equated with a new man, and to extend the symbolism, Shane also unhalters his horse and puts it out to pasture. The true cowhand never unhalters his horse while on the range. But Shane is no longer on the range. With his new clothes and his unhaltered horse, he now represents a new man.

In spite of that fact, however, young Bob recognizes that there is still something contradictory about Shane. While Shane is "no longer a dark stranger" and even though Shane was helping Joe Starrett farm, Shane is not a farmer and "never really could be." Bob distinctly feels that whatever Shane does, Shane is always "a man apart."

Bob's question to his father – "Could you beat Shane? In a fight, I mean" – is a typical question for a young boy to ask his father, but here it serves as a means for Joe to comment upon Shane's unique qualities – that is, some men have dynamite inside them; what Shane lacks in size and strength, he makes up for in "quickness of movement" and in "instinctive coordination of mind and muscle." Shane possesses a fierce energy and a driving intensity. These are the very qualities that we will later see in action during the barroom brawl, when Shane is pitted alone against five of Fletcher's roughnecks.

More mystery is added to Shane's character when we see him occupy Joe's chair at the dining table and when we notice that Shane always sits opposite a door so as to see who enters. It is a part of his "fixed alertness," in the same way that he is always aware of anyone approaching before others are aware of it. This suggests, of course, that Shane is tense about being caught unaware, that he is constantly expecting some sort of ambush.

Furthermore, Shane avoids company. While he is comfortable with the Starrett family, and while he is courteous to the other homesteaders, he is still withdrawn, always keeping a distance between himself and others. He recognizes that other homesteaders can never measure up to Joe, and that only Joe Starrett is a true leader of men.

Part of Shane's aloofness is correlated with his refusal to carry a gun. Shane is a very private man with very valid and private reasons for not carrying a gun. This fact confuses young Bob, because when he finds Shane's gun, he recognizes it as a magnificent and beautiful weapon, one that should be shown off. The fact that it is highly polished and that the hammer has been filed to a fine point confuses Bob, but alert readers should recognize that this is the gun of a professional gunshooter, of an expert. Joe Starrett confirms our opinion when he theorizes that Shane is an outstanding marksman – that he could shoot off Bob's button and Bob would feel nothing except the breeze.

Joe's final advice to his son at the end of the chapter foreshadows the end of the novel. Joe tells Bob not to become too attached to Shane because Shane will be leaving one of these days. In other words, Shane's stay at the farm is a sort of interlude in his life; he will never remain a farmer. Joe's prediction is correct, because at the end of the novel, Shane rides off alone, leaving Bob Starrett with only the memories recorded here.

Chapter 5

This chapter is a type of interlude – there is little action, and the plot does not move forward. However, in this interlude, we learn that by working together, Joe and Shane accomplish so much that Joe is able to ride out of the valley to another ranch and return home with a half-dozen more cattle. While Joe is gone, Shane posts a new section of the corral, making it half again as big, and later, he helps Joe herd the new cattle into it. One day, young Bob is playing with a gun, and Shane teaches him how to use it properly. Then suddenly, the summer is over.

Seemingly, this chapter is simple, but its simplicity should not allow the reader to underestimate its importance. It is important that we learn that Shane has become a part of the Starrett family and that there exists such a close comradeship between him and Joe that working together, they get much more accomplished. This is expressed best by Shane's using the plural pronoun "we" when referring to things about the farm.

When Joe returns with the half-dozen new cattle, he is so astonished to see the new corral that he momentarily forgets the cattle, and they begin to disperse. Instantly, Shane vaults onto Joe's horse and herds the cattle into the corral. Again, this incident emphasizes that Shane is an excellent horseman and an expert in herding cattle. Bob describes Shane in the most classic of all western terminology: "He was tall and straight in the saddle."

This particular summer is the perfect idyllic existence for young Bob: "I think that was the happiest summer of my life," he remembers. Here we have the classic situation of a paradise, a Garden of Eden image that is flawed only by the threat of the serpent in the person of Fletcher, or more accurately, Fletcher's "shadow," because Fletcher himself is away most of the summer, and Fletcher's cowhands are friendly when he isn't there to goad them.

Until Shane arrived, young Bob used his father as the ideal role model, and he also had Fletcher's friendly cowhands as role models; but now, with the arrival of Shane, Bob wants to be "more and more . . . like Shane, like the man I imagined he was in the past." In fact, Bob tells us, he listened with something "closely akin to worship" when Shane and his father talked. He was impressed that Shane agreed that Joe's method of raising cattle was superior to Fletcher's method – yet, still, there was "something," something mysterious and unspoken about Shane. One knew that Shane could never be a farmer permanently.

While young Bob is playing with an old gun one day, Shane steps forward and becomes the boy's teacher and mentor. During the course of the instruction, the reader learns that Shane is an expert on all matters pertaining to guns: he knows how various gunfighters carry their guns, how some even carry two guns, but Shane tells Bob, "that's a show-off stunt and a waste of weight. One's enough, if you know how to use it." This statement will later apply to the gunfighter, Stark Wilson; in the final shootout, Wilson will draw two guns against Shane but Shane's one gun is enough to defeat Wilson.

During the course of Shane's instructions on how to handle a gun, Bob notices that Shane's hands are different – that his hands know how to handle a gun, that his "hands seemed to have an intelligence all their own." Note too that Shane's final demonstration – tossing a gun, catching it, and aiming it – shows Bob (and us) that Shane is something of a showman. In addition, his instructions on aiming and shooting reveal that he is well versed in using a gun for killing.

Suddenly in the midst of the lesson to Bob, Shane's hands whiten and his entire attitude changes. He does not even hear Bob calling him: "He was back somewhere along the dark trail of the past." It is obvious that Shane has a bitter and painful past that he can't forget. Something from the past intrudes upon the present, making Shane a mysterious man with something ominous in his past life that we will never know about.

Recovering from his dark thoughts of the past, Shane gives Bob a final lesson: "a gun is as good – and as bad – as the man who carries it." By analogy, both Shane and his gun are good. At least in our view, Shane uses his gun only for the proper reasons.

Chapter 6

In this chapter, the conflict between the cattle baron (Luke Fletcher) and the homesteaders (led by Joe Starrett) is quickly coming to a climax. With the arrival of fall, Fletcher returns to the valley, carrying with him a contract to deliver all the beef he can for the next year. Not surprisingly, Fletcher believes that he needs the full range. We also learn that there is no marshal for a hundred miles, and even if there were a sheriff, he would be one of Fletcher's men because Fletcher is the power in the valley. The homesteaders agree that Fletcher is not the type of man to stoop to murder, but he has never been tested as he is being tested now. Of all the men in the valley, Fletcher dislikes Joe Starrett the most, and after Starrett, Fletcher hates Shane because Shane is working for Joe.

One day when Shane takes a broken piece of the haying

machine to town to be welded, he encounters Chris, one of Fletcher's men, who tries to provoke Shane into fighting. Shane essentially ignores him, even when young Chris mentions that it's obvious that farmers raise pigs—not cattle—because they *smell like pigs.* Everyone is surprised that Shane ignores the remark and returns to the farm.

The conflict between the cattle baron and the homesteaders is presented in its simplest statement: Fletcher "had his contract [and] the homesteaders would have to go." There is seemingly no recourse to legal action because this is the real frontier. The closest marshal is a hundred miles away, and thus, this country functions as a law unto itself. The "law of the six gun" will rule, and since Fletcher is the power in the valley, there is no one except Joe Starrett who dares to defy him. The other homesteaders, such as Lew Johnson and Henry Shipstead, are good people; those such as Frank Torrey and Ernie Wright are nervous, lazy, fidgety people. In addition, Ernie has a quick temper which will later be the cause of his death. Therefore, the only real "man" among the homesteaders in the valley is Joe Starrett, and because he is the strongest, he is the spokesman and an enemy of Fletcher. This is a case in which the worth of a man is known by the enemies he makes.

Shane hears talk about young Morley, who was attacked by Fletcher's men and returned bruised and beaten, cursed Joe and rode away. For Joe to hire another man, Shane, is a direct slap in the face to Fletcher. Clearly, "Shane was a marked man," and yet Bob tells us that it didn't matter because "He was Shane." In other words, nothing more needs to be said.

Bob also succinctly states the central conflict: "The issue in our valley was plain and would in time have to be pushed to a showdown. If Shane could be driven out, there would be a break in the homestead ranks, a defeat going beyond the loss of a man into the realm of prestige and morals. It would be the crack in the dam that would weaken the entire structure and finally let through the flood." As a result, some type of showdown is inevitable. Shane will not run, though, and he will prove to be equal to the task ahead of him.

The first confrontation occurs when young Chris, from Fletcher's ranch, sees Shane and Bob leave the Starrett farm in the wagon. He follows them to town, and he is accompanied by another ranchhand, but when this new man sees Shane, he leaves the country. Even though the new man says absolutely nothing about Shane or his reasons for leaving, his silence in addition to his abrupt, instant departure says a great deal. We gather that he isn't by nature a coward, but he is afraid of Shane. Therefore, he leaves as quickly as possible.

In the saloon – the typical setting for any western fight – Chris begins goading Shane and insulting Shane's manhood. Chris tosses out such insults as "this farmer drinks whiskey. I didn't think these plow-pushing dirt-grubbers drank anything stronger than soda pop." The insult results from one of the traditional standards of the West – that is, a "man" was defined as a free-riding, rough, whiskey-drinking cowpoke and not a fenced-in farmer. Shane is able to handle these types of comments good-naturedly, but when the insults become more underhanded – such as Chris' referring to the smell of the farmers being that of the dirty barnyard – Shane finds it difficult to withhold his furor. Ordering a soda pop for Bob, he leaves, fearful that he may lose his temper. Even Mr. Grafton, the owner of the saloon, realizes that Shane is afraid – not of Chris but of himself, his own temper. Nonetheless, Chris' first encounter with Shane causes Chris to foolhardedly spread the story of "the dirty pig farmers" around the valley, thereby forcing a second confrontation with Shane.

Chapter 7

In *Shane*, each chapter often deals with one central episode, along with other side, or tangential, matters. For example, Chapter 6 presented the first encounter between Shane and Chris, Fletcher's young cowhand, focusing on Shane's refusal to fight with Chris. This incident leads to the central event of

Chapter 7, and we see here the result of Shane's refusal to fight. Now, because of what has happened since Chapter 6, Shane realizes that he has no choice. He must fight young Chris.

To return to that first encounter, however, to see how the events in Chapter 7 came to pass, we should note that after Shane's refusal to fight, Fletcher quickly took advantage of the situation. For example, Fletcher's ranchhands began using the upper ford, which should have been for the homesteaders' use. In addition, the ranchhands made every effort to ride close to the homesteaders' property and shout insulting remarks about pigs and pig farmers until even Joe Starrett could hardly control himself. Therefore, whereas we previously applauded Shane's restraint – his refusal to resort to brutality and violence – we now see that his simple, human refusal to fight is responsible for the harsh and unpleasant pain that he is causing all the homesteaders, especially Joe Starrett.

The behavior of Fletcher's men is crude, coarse, and "silly for grown men," yet these men do not really know Shane and cannot be sure that Shane did not avoid the fight with Chris because of cowardice. Ultimately, the other homesteaders gather at Joe's place to complain that they can't even go to town because of everyone's contempt; even the neutral townspeople blame the situation on Shane ("They resented that he [Shane] was linked to them").

Shane realizes that he must do something – not just because of the homesteaders' complaints, but because he, Shane, works for Joe and is causing Joe to lose the respect and authority that he once held. Henry Shipstead expresses the feeling of all the homesteaders when he says to Joe: "I'm beginning to doubt your judgment." When the men argue that "You [Joe] can't dodge it" and point out that "your man's responsible," Shane knows that he must restore respect to Joe because "he did care what they thought of father."

The confrontation scene between Shane and Chris is part of classic western American literature. In addition, this barroom fight is a prelude to the more important barroom brawl in

Chapter 9. This minor fight – hardly a fight at all but more a device to establish Shane's authority and power – functions to effectively put an end to the unpleasant rumors about the homesteaders and about their (nonexistent) pigs. As Shane says afterward to the farmers when he returns to the Starretts' place: "Your pigs are dead and buried." Here, we should note that Shane is not pleased with himself; he has lost that sense of serenity that came to him during the summer. Furthermore, Shane says that "he could have liked" young Chris – if it hadn't been for the feud.

The actual fight between Shane and Chris is narrated secondhand. Our narrator (young Bob) is reporting what another homesteader, Ed Howells, told the group. In the next big barroom brawl, young Bob will be there in person to report the fight.

Concerning the fight in this chapter, it is a one-sided affair. Young Chris never has a chance. First, he is humiliated by being slapped several times, and when he tries to attack Shane, Shane annihilates him, hurtling Chris over, snapping his arm and cracking the bone. But suddenly, something unexpected happens. Shane quietly scoops up the wounded boy, cradles him in his arms, and lays him on a table. Then he gently administers to him, wiping off the blood and tending to him. It is interesting that at the time of this novel, 1949, the term "macho" did not exist. Yet Fletcher and Chris are typically "macho" types – conspicuously cruel and proud, afraid to exhibit any sensitivity for fear that it might tarnish their aggressive "masculinity." Shane defies the fraudulent swaggering stereotype and proves that a "manly" man can also be gentle and caring. After he thoroughly trounces Chris, Shane shows an unexpected, extraordinary tenderness toward the young antagonist. At the end of the chapter, Marian shows an unusually perceptive ability, and at the end of the next chapter, Shane will tell Marian that she is a very discerning woman. When Marian expresses a fear that Joe has made a mistake because of what happened, Joe thinks that Marian is concerned for young Chris. Marian, however, is more perceptive; she is concerned with what Joe has done to Shane – that is, the conflict in the valley has aroused things in Shane that should have remained dormant.

Chapter 8

The fears that Marian expressed at the end of Chapter 7 are verified here in Chapter 8. The serenity that Shane found during his summer's work is now gone. Shane is now "restless with some far hidden desperation." He becomes the loner again, disappearing from the house after supper, and when Bob seeks him out, he is usually standing alone, isolated and looking out over the vast expanse of land.

In brief, Chapter 8 presents the effect of Shane's fight on Bob and on Marian. First, when Bob asks Shane if he can teach him how to fight, Shane says that fighting like he did can't be learned. Then he tries to justify his fight. He gave young Chris every opportunity to avoid fighting and still keep his self-respect; Chris could have called it off, and he could have done it "without crawling . . . if he was man enough." Shane desperately wants Bob to understand this principle, and Bob tells us that, to please Shane, he told him that he did understand. But as Bob reports later, he was too young to comprehend what Shane meant. Thus, Bob, the mature narrator, is able to show us the differences between the world of the adult and the world of the child. Bob reports what he did not understand when he was young, but we the readers do understand what Shane is trying to say. As Bob the mature man writes: "It was a long, long time before I did [understand] it and then I was a man myself and Shane was not there for me to tell."

The last scene in this chapter employs a narrative technique that is frowned upon by most writers. Bob is eavesdropping on a private conversation which he reports to us even though he does not understand the conversation. This is an amateurish narrative technique, but it is used by Schaefer in order to convey the private conversation between Shane and Marian to the reader.

In this conversation, as noted in the last chapter, we discover how perceptive and discerning Marian is when she confronts Shane and asks him if he is planning to move on. She asks him not to go because Joe needs him. And then to confirm the earlier allusions made to the sexual attraction between them, she admits that she also needs him, even though it would be easier for her "if [Shane] rode out of this valley and never came back" because she would not be tempted by his masculine appeal. But she does point out how desperately Shane is needed. Without Shane, all will fail. When Shane promises her that "You'll not lose this place," we know Shane well enough now that we are certain that if Shane says that he will do something, he will do it.

Chapter 9

This chapter presents the central fight scene in the novel. In fact, this barroom brawl or fight scene might be considered the standard by which all western fight scenes should be measured. It is certainly the best fight scene to be found in western American literature.

Before the fight scene, however, we readers are lulled into a false sense of serenity. The chapter begins, "Another period of peace had settled over our valley." But note that in spite of the calm, Joe and Shane make it a point to always work together, and now Joe always carries his gun, even in the field, because both Joe and Shane know that there is more trouble to come. Young Bob is not yet mature enough to know this.

A typical trip to town on Saturday night is presented next, but on this particular night, Joe and Marian have to stay later in order to talk to Bob's teacher, Jane Grafton. This is a situation which will allow Shane to go into the saloon. Once Shane is in there, five of Fletcher's men come in, led by the heavyset, burly Morgan. They attack Shane and beat him almost to a pulp before Joe is able to come to Shane's help, and then, when only Morgan is left, Shane takes him on in a one-to-one fight which leaves Morgan prostrate on the saloon floor.

The contrast between the opening of this chapter, with the

emphasis on quiet serenity and on civilized matters, on simple chores such as buying necessary provisions, and on talking chit-chat is brilliant. It is also ironic that Joe and Marian's concern for Bob's schooling and thus, for civilizing him, leads Joe far away from the saloon, where a fiercely barbaric, anti-civilized savage fight is about to take place. In a sense, Bob's playing hooky and going fishing causes Shane to be alone and unde-fended against an overwhelming number of opponents.

Before the fight takes place, Bob sees Red Marlin walk into the saloon, and he violates his parents' dictate and goes into the forbidden bar and warns Shane that there are others out-side waiting for him. Shane, however, calmly asks: "Bobby boy, would you have me run away?" This question evokes in Bob a deep and abiding love for this man, a love so deep that it will be remembered forever; merely knowing someone like Shane has become an event so incredible and so momentous and so memorable that it leaves the boy forever touched by his con-tact. At that moment, as remembered by Bob the adult man, Shane meant everything to Bob: "Love for that man raced through me and the warmth ran down and stiffened my legs and I was so proud of being there with him that I could not keep the tears from my eyes."

In the fight scene in this chapter, the strength and power of the narration holds the reader breathless and spellbound as we rush forward to discover the outcome of the fight. The nar-rative excellence of this fight scene is the criteria by which other western fight scenes are measured, and as is befitting of the typical western novel, the fight takes place in a saloon with a background of smoke, poker chips, and cheap whiskey. (Many westerns will vary the setting – some will have the fight occur in the road in front of the saloon – but this is a mere variation on the basic saloon setting.)

The odds in the fight are overwhelmingly against Shane. The appearance of the men is captured in the image of an army phalanx: "Morgan was in the lead now with his men spread out behind him." Shane is trapped by this solid bulk of manpower descending on him. First, there are five against one, but Shane flips Morgan, and it is four against one. Then, when he knees another in the crotch, it is three against one, and when Morgan recovers it is again four against one. Through it all, Shane is the valiant underdog who moves with lightning-fast strokes against the laborious, lumbering attacks of the ranchhands, who are slow and clumsy compared to Shane and who use dirty and unfair tactics. When one man jumps up and kicks Shane with his feet, Curly and Red Marlin are able to pin Shane down while Morgan cowardly breaks a bottle over Shane's head. Then with the others "bravely" holding Shane, Morgan begins to pound him with blows to his head. But Joe suddenly comes to the rescue, and this is a new Joe — a Joe we have not seen, who we didn't even know existed. Joe, seeing Shane trapped with blood streaming from him, becomes a man of rage and fury. He hurls the big, burly Morgan aside and picks up Curly as though Curly were a sack of potatoes. Joe lifts Curly above his head and hurls him crashing across the room. When Red Marlin sees what is happening, he runs for the door: "His flight was frantic, head-long."

As Joe goes to finish Morgan off, Shane calls to him: "Wait, Joe. The man's mine." The contrast in this final fight should be obvious. Whereas Morgan and four others ganged up on Shane, and whereas Joe and Shane would be justified in the two of them taking on Morgan, yet their honorable natures will not entertain such a cowardly manner of fighting. Thus, Shane will take on Morgan on a one-to-one basis. This is expressed by Bob in another of his understatements when he knows that Shane will win because "he was Shane." No more needs to be said.

In the fight against Morgan, even the most nonviolent reader secretly relishes and anticipates the thrashing which Shane will give him. And throughout the fight, Morgan resorts to every type of dirty tactic that he can think of, but through it all, Shane, although he is severely hurt, remains ever-alert and agile, circling and dodging the hulking Morgan, while repeatedly getting short fist stabs into him.

Even though this novel was published in the late 1940s, the contemporary reader will recognize Shane's fighting technique as resembling those of modern karate – that is, he allows his body to roll, and he catches Morgan with his feet and sends him flying against the wall; another time, he uses his hands opened like boards, slashing into his opponent's neck at a strategic angle. Through it all, Shane moves "like a flame among them." He whirls and then plunges backward. He is always incredibly quick and elusive. Schaefer's mark as a superior writer lies in these scenes which totally involve the reader.

Chapter 10

As has been a pattern throughout the novel, we have a big action scene, which is then followed by a scene showing the after-effects of the previous action. Here, after Shane has beaten Morgan, we see him in the quietness that has now settled in the saloon, and for the first time, we see "how battered and bloody he was," whereas during the fight, Bob reports that "you saw only the splendor of movement, the flowing brute beauty of line and power in action." Now comes the realization that Shane has taken bitter punishment.

One of the townsmen, Mr. Weir, comes forward to help, but Shane will receive no help from anyone except Joe Starrett. As Joe goes to help Shane, Shane collapses in Joe's arms. The image of Shane as a child being cradled in Joe's big arms reminds Bob of how Joe used to carry him to bed.

Later, at home, Marian administers to Shane's wounds with tenderness and love. The family is united, and yet there is an under-tension, and Joe lets Marian know that he is aware that there is an attraction between her and Shane. Joe says, "Do you think I don't know, Marian?" and Marian understands his reference is to her feeling for Shane, and she counters that "You don't [know]. You can't. Because I don't know myself." Again, Bob reports these events, acknowledging that they are a part of "that adult knowledge beyond [his] understanding."

Chapter 11

This chapter presents the next significant development, as well as the most deadly, with the appearance of the hired gunslinger, Stark Wilson. But even before his appearance, it is evident that matters in the valley have changed. From Bob's point of view, everything seems to be going fine because Fletcher and his men leave them alone after the big fight. But this is a false sense of security because the men are constantly guarding against any type of outbreak. While Bob feels that "all this caution failed to make sense to me," the men are more wary than ever. They know that the struggle has only begun. They explain to Bob that Fletcher has gone too far to back out now, and he has to force the homesteaders out now, or else he will be the one to be forced out of the valley. The struggle becomes a desperate struggle – a struggle for simple survival. The valley can no longer hold both the homesteaders and the cattle baron.

Fletcher's absence from the valley creates a further aura of suspense and suspicion. Shane is more aware than ever that Fletcher will be looking for some way more forceful and more certain than a mere barroom brawl, and as reported by Lew Johnson, Fletcher has brought back from Cheyenne a hired, two-gun professional killer who has a reputation for already having killed a number of people in Kansas and the Southwest territories. Wilson is said to be "just as good with either hand and as fast on the draw as the best of them." This established, well-known killer with an infamous reputation will be Shane's opponent.

We should now remember that, in Shane's opinion, a two-gun killer is not necessarily as efficient as, or as accurate as, a one-gun fighter. One should remember this statement – particularly during the showdown between Shane and Wilson; there, we will see Shane's skill with his one gun. The conflict is now reaching the point where either Shane – or one of Fletcher's men – must kill or be killed.

In our admiration of Shane, we should not overlook the fact that Stark Wilson is dressed in a manner that is very similar to the way that Shane was dressed when he first appeared in the valley. Note also that the name "Stark" describes the kind of person that he is. Stark Wilson is starkly dressed in stark black clothes, and his behavior is unwaveringly stark. Both Wilson and Shane wear dark matching pants and a coat made out of fine, but worn, material. The main outward difference is that Stark Wilson wears two guns strapped to his legs while Shane has only one gun, which he keeps wrapped up and hidden.

As soon as Shane hears about the arrival of the hired killer, he immediately wants Lew Johnson to bring whoever has the "hottest head" or whoever is "the easiest to prod into being a fool" to the Starretts' farm. Shane's action indicates that he knows a professional killer is not going to sit around; a professional killer will immediately take some action to assert his superiority to the local farmers. Unfortunately, Shane is absolutely correct. Frank Torrey quickly brings the news that Ernie Wright has just been shot and killed by the professional killer.

For the third time, the narrator is not Bob but an outside narrator; earlier, Chris and Shane's fight was reported by Ed Howells, and the arrival of the gunslinger was reported by Lew Johnson. Torrey tells how the gunslinger goaded Ernie into committing himself before Ernie realized the significance of what he had done. Again, as happened in the saloon fight scene, Schaefer's powerful narrative force carries the reader along. We are deeply involved because our sense of justice is outraged by this obvious travesty of justice – this set-up to force the homesteaders to sell their land to Fletcher, or else Fletcher will target his hired gunslinger on the person refusing to sell.

The homesteaders are frightened and rightly so. They are exposed to the law of the Old West, where the fastest man on the draw wins, and there are no questions asked. But as Lewis says: "What chance have any of us got against Wilson? We're not gunmen. We're just a bunch of old cowhands and farmers." Jim calls it murder, and Shane agrees with him, pointing out, "It's murder. Trick it out as self-defense or with fancy words about an even break for a fair draw and it's still murder." Shane apparently knows what he is talking about because, we gather, he has been in such a situation before, and he knows about it first-hand.

The conflict then is drawn between the homesteaders who represent the forces of civilization and the cattle baron/rancher who represents the barbaric law of "every man for himself and the fastest man on the draw wins." It is a fight in which one individual cannot murder another without fear of punishment.

Shane further analyzes the situation and determines that Fletcher and his killer won't bother any of the other homesteaders. Fletcher, he says, will concentrate on Joe because without Joe, all the others would immediately pick up and leave. Shane then pours accolades on Joe, "the one real man in the valley," and thus the only man whom Fletcher has to deal with. Bob sums it up as follows: "They would stay as long as father was there. With him gone, Fletcher would have things his way."

Joe realizes how much depends on him, and when he tells Marian that "there are some things a man can't take. Not if he's to go on living with himself," there is suddenly a significant change in Shane. Not only does Bob notice it, but so does Joe.

Shane's old hidden desperation comes descending back upon him—some terrible torment from the past now confronts him again. This change in Shane bothers Joe immensely because Joe does not want to get Shane involved in a life-or-death conflict. Joe feels that Shane "won his fight before he ever came riding into this valley," and for the sake of not committing Shane to some violent action, because of his respect and love for Shane and his past, for the sake of Shane's battles with others and more important with himself, Joe is willing to make the ultimate sacrifice—selling out—so as not to involve Shane in their dreadful conflict. He cannot sacrifice such a magnificent man as Shane; he would prefer to sell out.

Marian, who has proved that she possesses the strong independent will of a good frontier woman, argues against her husband. She feels that they must live up to Shane's ideal conception of them. They can't let him down. Finally, Joe agrees with

Marian; if they leave this place, "the salt would be gone." There would be no pleasure in life.

Chapter 12

The central episode in this short chapter is the meeting between Joe and Luke Fletcher, during which we hear Fletcher's surprising offer. At the beginning of the chapter, Joe and Shane have been in town at Ernie Wright's funeral, and Marian and Bob have whiled away the time on the farm playing several games of Parcheesi. The key effect of the funeral is to draw together many people who did not even know Ernie; clearly, the townspeople are repulsed by Fletcher's underhanded methods. They don't want a gunslinger in their valley.

The arrival of Fletcher at the Starretts' farm, accompanied by Stark Wilson and two cowhands, is not unexpected because Joe knows that Fletcher has read the temper of the town and knows that he must act quickly. This is the reader's first direct knowledge of Fletcher. Until now, Fletcher has been a distant and abstract force of evil. We are somewhat surprised to discover that he is a tall man, once handsome, with a finely chiseled face. In contrast, Stark Wilson seems serene and deadly.

When Joe demands to know Fletcher's intent, Fletcher can't help but be insulting when he refers to the homesteaders as "nesters," a derogatory term. Then he catches everyone offguard by offering to buy the Starrett place and by offering Joe and Shane good jobs on his ranch. Fletcher is getting rid of Morgan, he says, and he would like Joe to be his new foreman and Shane to be his new trail boss.

Joe asks Shane if he can answer for both of them. When Shane agrees, Joe asks Fletcher what is to happen to the other homesteaders. When Joe hears that they will have to go, he rejects Fletcher's offer. Fletcher is prepared for this rejection; he warns Joe in a thinly veiled threat that what happened to Ernie could happen to him, and then he plants a trap for Joe, telling him to think about it until tonight and then meet him at Grafton's place—on neutral grounds. Before Joe answers,

Fletcher rides off. The purpose of the meeting, of course, is obvious to all concerned. There will be a trap of some sort for Joe to fall into so that he will have to draw against the gun-slinger, Stark Wilson, and Joe will, of course, be killed by Wilson.

After Fletcher leaves, the hired killer remains long enough to toss out some insults to Joe concerning Marian—saying that if Joe doesn't sell, "someone else [will] be enjoying this place of yours—and that woman there in the window." The meaning is obvious: if Joe doesn't sell, he will be killed and someone else will be married to or bedding down with his wife. This is a tremendous insult because the true western man does not allow, nor does he tolerate, a stranger, or any man, to make a slur-ring reference to his wife. A husband is duty-bound to protect his wife's honor. Thus, Joe has been placed in an impossible situation. He knows that he can't outdraw Wilson, but at the same time, he can't sit back and allow his wife to be insulted and his property to be confiscated.

Chapter 13

As mentioned before, the previous chapter presented Fletcher's sudden appearance at the Starretts' place and his un-expected offer to Joe and his challenge to meet Joe at Grafton's; this chapter, then, shows the effect of Fletcher's offer and Shane's resolution to take things into his own hands.

After Fletcher's departure, Joe, Marian, and Shane sit in absolute stillness. "They knew that Fletcher had dealt himself a winning hand," and each one of them knows that the other knows the situation exactly—that is, as noted in the discussion of Chapter 12, Joe will be drawn into an argument with Fletcher, the killer will become involved, and Joe will be forced to draw against the killer and be killed. While the boy does not fully grasp all of the implications, even he is aware of how life has changed completely because of Shane and Shane's influence: "Everything that had happened before seemed far off, almost like another existence."

Joe, of course, is deeply troubled because he knows that he can't beat Wilson to the draw and will be killed, but he knows that he has the strength in his powerful body to remain standing long enough to kill Wilson afterward. But he is troubled as to what will happen afterward to Marian and Bob. His mind is somewhat relieved, however, because he knows that his family "will be in better hands than his own"—that is, Shane will move in and take his place.

Shane's reaction to this statement is sharp and instantaneous: "His hands were clenched tightly . . . arms quivering. . . . He was desperate with an inner torment, his eyes tortured . . ." Obviously, Shane has never been confronted with such a predicament. First, Joe's assumption that Shane will take his place and settle down with his family is alien to Shane's nature. Even though Shane cares for Marian and Bob, Shane could never settle down. As he says later, farming has been something of a game he has played and played well, but he is by nature a wanderer, a drifter, and a loner. In addition, Shane is stunned by the moral horror of again having to kill another man; after all, he has no personal grudge against Wilson. It would be an impersonal killing. Shane is also disturbed by the dread of having to re-enter the world of violence.

Bob sees Shane looking out over the farm, and he realizes that a very definite change is coming over Shane. It is as though in seeing the farm, Shane takes on a new attitude and a new resolve. He puts past reservations behind him. He is now ready to face the challenge of the present; this is clear when he suddenly appears "framed in the doorway," wearing his gun. He is dressed in his matching pants and coat outfit, with his black hat—the outfit of a gunslinger. Note especially the image of Shane "framed in the doorway." This is an image that has appeared in an untold number of western novels and movies.

When Bob sees Shane wearing his gun, he realizes that Shane is now complete—the gun, the belt, and the holster are "a part of [Shane], part of the man, of the full sum of the integrate force that was Shane." In other words, this scene re-emphasizes that Shane has merely been playing at being a farmer. Now, wearing his gun, he is back in his own territory, and he is now the dangerous man whom we previously heard of.

When Joe tells Shane that the conflict with Fletcher involves only himself ("it's my business"), Shane corrects him and says, "This is my business." In other words, when Joe says "my business," he means what is about to happen is his concern, whereas Shane means that the "business" of confronting a killer is the type of business that he knows best. Shane points out the difference when he says, "I've had fun being a farmer," but when it comes to a shootout, a farmer such as Joe has no business being involved. Shane has enjoyed working at being a farmer — being a part of civilizing the frontier — but now he is back in his real place, his real element, back in the real world that he knows. It is a world that Joe doesn't know, and Shane must take control of the dreaded business at hand. To do so, Shane must resort to knocking Joe out so as to save Joe from being killed by Wilson or from interfering with Shane's purpose.

Shane leaves Marian and Bob to tell Joe that he need not be "ashamed of being beat by Shane." It is almost as though Shane were boasting, but actually, it is the statement of a man who knows his own worth and has pride in his ability. Shane is "stating a fact, simple and elemental as the power that dwelled in him."

Since Shane and Marian have avoided speaking about their own feelings, about their possible love for one another, now Marian brings up the subject when she asks Shane if he is doing this (meeting the killer) "just for me?" Surveying the entire farm — including Marian, Joe and Bob — Shane cannot separate one part from another. He is meeting this challenge for them all, for all things combined.

Chapter 14

This chapter presents the dramatic climax of the novel — the showdown between Shane and Wilson — and the resulting shootout. Realizing that this is the climactic shootout, Bob is determined to miss nothing. Following Shane, Bob sees him take his saddle-roll, an act which foreshadows Shane's plans to leave the valley. He hears Shane whistle for his horse, and in true western idiom, his horse comes to him immediately. Then, Bob, in rather exaggerated, fanciful language, sees Shane as "tall and terrible" in the saddle – "the symbol of all the dim, formless imaginings of danger and terror in the untested realm of human potentialities beyond my understanding."

Upon arriving at the saloon, Shane enters through the typically western swinging doors, an image that occurs in an untold number of westerns. He stands and surveys the saloon. The entire shootout, as is to be expected, is set against the most typical of all western scenes: the saloon, the poker table and the poker chips, the bar and the whiskey and the half-smoked cigars, and of major importance, the little balcony from which Fletcher will treacherously shoot at Shane's back.

As young Bob watches, Shane becomes everything that the boy has ever, even in his wildest imagination, conceived of Shane as being: "This was the Shane of the adventures I had dreamed for him, cool and competent, facing that room full of men in the simple solitude of his own invincible completeness." This, then, is young Bob's idealized version of his idol, and, consequently, this perfection cannot be tarnished. Thus, after the fight, even as magnificent as Shane was, the boy must be reassured that Shane's wound was not because of his idol's lack of perfection, but only because of his lack of practice.

As Shane is looking for Fletcher, he encounters Wilson instead. Apparently, Fletcher is hiding. When Shane heads for the door in search of Fletcher, he finds his way and the door blocked by Wilson. The two gunshooters are facing each other. Shane is in the inferior position because Wilson has maneuvered in such a way that Shane is in the middle of the floor while Wilson's back is protected by a wall of the saloon. Earlier, we saw that Shane always wanted to be against the wall – that is, he never wanted his back exposed. Shane "did not like the setup. Wilson had the front wall and he [Shane] was left in the open of the room." But Shane assesses his position and accepts it.

For Wilson, things have taken a dramatic change. He has come to the valley to kill Joe Starrett. After he killed Ernie Wright, Wilson cannot conceive that there could possibly be anyone in this valley who would dare to stand up to him. The fact that there is someone – a Shane, who tells him, "Your killing days are done" – astonishes Wilson. He realizes that Shane is no Ernie Wright. As a professional killer, Wilson is accustomed to sizing up his opponents, and looking at Shane, he finds him "not to his liking." But true to his profession, he faces Shane in the shootout, and Shane beats him to the draw, wounds him, and as Wilson tries to shoot with his other gun, Shane finishes him off, but not before Shane himself has been wounded.

After the shootout, the ultimate treachery occurs. We have not been led to believe that Fletcher was such an evil man as to shoot a man in the back, but that is exactly what he plans to do. However, Shane whirls around after Fletcher shoots and misses, and in a single flash, he kills Fletcher before Fletcher has time to reload his gun.

Shane has triumphed. He has saved the valley, and even though he is wounded, he announces in classic western language that he will be "riding on now."

Bob, however, has noticed Shane's wound, and he has to follow Shane so as to have the full measure of his hero restored. He has to know that Shane could have easily outdrawn Wilson if Shane had been practicing during the summer. Shane, recognizing the boy's need for a hero, restores the boy's worship by agreeing with Bob. The idol is then restored to his pedestal, and Shane, dressed exactly as he was in the opening page (except then, he was without his gun), rides away into the distance, and "a cloud passed over the moon . . . and he was gone."

Chapters 15 & 16

Shane, of course, does not appear any more in the novel. These last two chapters present, as have the preceding ones, the effect that Shane's gunfight has upon the valley, and more particularly, upon the Starrett family. It is revealing to note that Joe is not surprised to hear that Shane killed Wilson. After all, "He was Shane." But Joe assumes that Shane was also killed in the shootout. Consequently, he is at a loss to know how to accept the news that Shane is still alive and that he has ridden out of the valley. While he is pondering these events, we see one of the first results of the shootout. Chris, the young cowhand whom Shane thought had the makings of a real man, comes to the Starretts to offer himself as a hired hand, confessing that he knows he is "a damned poor substitute" for Shane. Thus, even in his absence, Shane has made a real man of Chris.

Joe spends the night wandering around his farm looking at the changes that have been made as a result of Shane's having been there. At dawn, Marian and Bob find him out by the corral. Joe feels that because of the sacrifice Shane made, remaining in the valley wouldn't be the thing to do. He wants to pull up stakes and start over again, but Marian is firm. She points out that Shane is "all around" them and that it would be a betrayal to him if they left. She then challenges Joe to pull up one of the posts that Shane put in. It is so deep in the ground, however, that Joe, despite all of his tremendous bulk, cannot budge it. Marian tells him that because of Shane's work, they all have roots in this place. This image then takes a full turn because the novel opened with Shane helping cut the roots of the big stump which was a hindrance to civilizing the frontier. Now, Shane's fence posts represent the fences of civilization that he helped establish.

This final chapter is seen in terms of "the making of a myth." That is, as time goes by, stories about Shane begin to grow and spread, and other details are added to the stories. Bob never participates in these stories because he knows that Shane secretly belongs to him and his parents; if others want to make a myth or legend out of Shane, Bob is not concerned.

The final paragraph captures the mythic quality of Shane: "He was the man who rode into our little valley . . . and when his work was done," he rode away. "He was Shane."

CHARACTER ANALYSES

SHANE

From the first time he enters the valley and announces, "Call me Shane," until the end of the novel when no more needs to be said except, "He was Shane," this figure dominates the novel. He is the reason for the narration of the story. That is, the story of Shane is told by young Bob Starrett after Bob is grown because Shane is a part of an incredible and enduring moment in a boy's childhood. Shane has become a legend and a myth, a representation of something so enormous and so memorable as to never be forgotten. In other words, Shane appeared from out of nowhere, performed unbelievable feats of skill and courage, created a permanent impression upon the valley and especially on the boy, and then rode off into the distance.

Shane first appears in the valley wearing matching pants and a coat of worn elegance and a black dress hat, clothes that are traditionally associated with a gambler or with a gunslinger. This outfit is similar to the clothes that Stark Wilson will wear. But the clothes do not tell the entire story; behind the clothes, Bob Starrett immediately perceives a kind of magnificence, a unique type of strength and quality and competence. Shane inspires such confidence that, given the time and occasion, this man seems as if he could accomplish almost anything that he sets his mind to. Thus, from the very beginning, Shane becomes the idol, the hero, and the perfect example of the ideal man whom Bob wants to become.

Physically, Shane is rather slight; yet, despite his slim build, he is nevertheless very rugged, solid and compact. "What he lacked . . . in size and strength, he made up in quickness of movement, in instinctive coordination of mind and muscle and in that sudden fierce energy that burned in him." These qualities are those which will allow him to relentlessly attack the stump, as well as Chris, Morgan, and later, Stark Wilson. And in each encounter, Shane will emerge the victor.

In addition to the above virtues, Shane is also a rather

courteous and reserved person, soft-spoken and withdrawn to the point of being almost antisocial. Certainly, in his first encounter with Chris, his soft-spokenness leads other people in the valley to misinterpret his strength and will. Note, too, that throughout his association with the Starretts, Shane shows a sense of deep tenderness. As noted in the commentaries, Shane possesses a multiple-dimension machoism. That is, in his treatment of Bob, although there is something mysterious in Shane's background, a gentleness and a tenderness shine through his rough exterior. Likewise, after he has beaten Chris in a rough, manly fight, Shane exercises great tenderness in caring for the young man's bruises, thus illustrating the two qualities of true manliness — toughness combined with tenderness.

Shane is the patient teacher, taking painstaking efforts to show young Bob some of the tricks of shooting, and advising him how to keep his eyes open and alert. He often talks to Bob as though Bob were a grown man, especially after the fight with Chris, when Shane wants to let Bob know that the fight was not necessary — that Chris could have withdrawn. In teaching Bob how to handle a gun, how to ride "tall and straight in the saddle," and the concept that fighting is not learned — that it comes naturally — Bob learns all sorts of things about Shane. He learns that Shane is an expert marksman, that Shane is an expert horseman, and during one lesson, Bob becomes aware of Shane's hands; they seem "to have an intelligence all their own."

Shane is finally evaluated, to a great extent, by the effect which he has on other people. The effect on young Bob is inestimable; in fact, it is so great that years later Bob will write this book about his memories of Shane. Shane's effect on Joe and Marian extends from the trivial (his ability to bring out Joe's natural talkativeness and Marian's deep desire to please through her cooking) to such an important decision as the Starretts' decision to remain in the valley — because Shane has made his presence felt in every part of their homestead, from the removal of the stump to the building of the corral and to the embedding of the fence posts. Finally, Shane has a significant effect on the entire valley because Shane not only has influenced young Chris to ask to work for Joe, but as a result of Shane's brief stay, the entire valley is now a peaceful and law-abiding valley. All of this happens because "He was Shane."

JOE STARRETT

Joe was once a cowhand. Now he is a farmer, and he is proud of being a farmer. He deliberately chose to "quit punching cattle for another man's money" and to establish a part of the West as his land and his family's home. Joe represents the forces of civilization that are trying to tame the frontier, or the wilderness, and the open plains. As such, Joe's philosophy will be diametrically opposed to the large cattle barons who need the open plains for grazing.

In contrast to Shane, Joe is a big man—a hulking, powerfully built man. He is not only physically big, but he is also big in the things that he represents and in his manner that keeps all of the homesteaders together. Joe Starrett is also a representative of the frontier spirit which wages war against the untamed land and brings civilization to that land. He is the natural family man whose love for and devotion to the family becomes tantamount in everything he does. Joe works for the sake of the family, providing them with basic necessities, with education and civilization, and with protection from harm and danger. He gives them a sense of security and belonging.

Shane expresses for the reader the difference between Joe and the other homesteaders. It is because Joe is so strong and so dominant that Fletcher wants to get to Joe. Shane knows that Fletcher and his crew will try to destroy Joe because, with Joe gone, the resolve of the remaining homesteaders will collapse. Shane says that Fletcher "picked Wright to make the play plain. That's done. Now he'll head straight for the one real man in this valley, the man who's held you here and will go on trying to hold you and keep for you what's yours as long as there's life in him . . ." and that man is Joe Starrett.

Although Joe is usually a gentle man, he turns into a howling fury if he is aroused. When he discovers that Shane is being held by two men while Morgan is pounding him with his fists, Joe appears in the room "big and terrible . . . he was filled with a fury that was shaking him almost beyond endurance." He takes Morgan out of the fight, picks up Curly as though Curly were a sack of potatoes and hurls him across the room. Yet, when the fight is over, Joe can, like Shane, show great tenderness, as he does in this scene for the battered and bloody Shane.

Joe's ultimate nobility comes when he is ready to sacrifice his own homestead so as not to involve Shane. Joe recognizes that Shane has fought a terrible personal battle with himself against some dark forces, and Joe does not want to reawaken those dark forces within Shane. Thus, although Joe is strong and powerful and dedicated, he is also sensitive to the feelings of others and is always fair and just.

MARIAN STARRETT

Marian represents the civilizing elements of New England. She is proud that her New England cooking exceeds the quality of others; her devotion to cooking represents in its own way her contribution to civilizing the frontier. For example, when Shane and Joe are chopping at the stump, the novel's key symbol of defiance to civilization, Marian sends out a pan of excellent biscuits, a symbol of the refinements of civilization. But Marian is not oblivious to the physical aspect of life. She is conscious of the physical brute strength of the two men, she is entranced by the brutal fight, she glories in the victory, and she is physically attracted to the slender but taut power in Shane's being.

Marian is also a discerning and perceptive woman. She knows that Shane is about to leave, and she asks him to stay because Joe needs him. She also implies enough to let Shane know that she also needs him. Later, she is able to point out to Joe that to leave the farm would be a betrayal to Shane — that because of his effort and his work on the farm, they are obligated to remain there. Of course, Marian is also the model woman of settled civilization speaking, the woman who does not want to pull up stakes and move elsewhere.

Essentially, Marian's role is that of the supportive frontier woman who is conscious of her femininity, and she is also proud to be a part of the settling of the West.

CRITICAL ESSAYS

Shane — Novel & Movie: A Comparison

Shane is a beautiful film; it won the Academy Award for best cinematography in spite of the fact that Paramount cut off the top and bottom of the picture in order for it to be shown on the new and fashionable wide-angle screen. The movie was also nominated for four other Academy Awards (Best Picture, Best Director, Best Supporting Actor, and Best Screenplay); since its release, *Shane* has become known as the classic American western film.

The film opens against a backdrop of the majestic and awesome Teton Mountains. A young boy is outside tracking down a deer, and framed through the slender antlers, Shane rides into the valley. Thus, Joey (Bob, in the novel) first sees his hero. The use of the antlers as a frame continues throughout the movie; later, the shadows of the antlers frame the sleeping Joey, and then as he awakens, the antlers make a frame around the boy's outside window. This image is continued later as Shane rides into town to meet Wilson, the gunslinger. There is a view of two slender saplings jutting out, antler-like, on a hill. Shane rides through these saplings on his way to meet Wilson. Another instance of the antler-like frame occurs at the Starretts' wedding anniversary, when Joe and Marian are framed by branches shaped like arches, or antlers.

The arrival of Shane in the film carries the same significance as it does in the novel. In the film, Shane rides out of the magnificent Tetons, and he is immediately (no delay, as in the novel) involved in the conflict in the valley. That is, Shane arrives at the moment that the conflict is coming to a climax, and he is presented as the god-like hero who will solve the conflict between the rancher and homesteader and bring peace and law and order to the troubled valley. But whereas the novel has Shane arrive in the worn elegance of a gunfighter's outfit, thus aligning him with such a profession, the movie has him arrive in a beautiful buckskin outfit, blond and all-American looking. However, the movie lets us quickly know that Shane is "gun wary"; when young Joey is playing with a gun, Shane jumps for his draw.

The movie tends to simplify the character of Shane, whereas the ambiguity in Shane's nature is forcefully depicted in the novel. As noted already, from the beginning of the movie, Shane's arrival in buckskin (instead of the darkly evil and foreboding matching pants and coat and black hat) aligns him to a more wholesome past in the film, as opposed to a dark and shady past in the novel. And whereas the novel constantly emphasizes that there is something mysterious and terrible in Shane's past from which he is escaping, these feelings are not present in the movie. The demonstration with the gun in the movie is an indication that Shane is an expert gunman, but it does not imply, as does the novel, that Shane might have used this expertise as a professional gunfighter.

As with the novel, the stump takes on symbolic significance, but rather than showing how the two men work with their own natural ability (Joe using his hulk and Shane using his agility), the movie, using a special camera technique, presents the two men in a symphony and harmony of movement.

Along with the conquering of the stump, the major conflict is introduced as Ryker (Fletcher) and his men ride through Marian's cultivated garden patch to throw the challenge to Joe; here (unlike the novel), Shane is immediately drawn into the conflict when he sides with Joe. The trampling of the vegetable garden emphasizes the conflict between the civilizing forces of the Starretts and the tyranny of the range, represented by Ryker.

In terms of abstract dialectics, or arguments, the movie allows Ryker to state convincingly the position of the ranchers, or the cattle barons. They were the ones who came here and braved the wild elements, fought with the Indians, and some were even wounded. Now, the homesteaders arrive – when things are safe – and they fence off part of the range and begin using the water supply. However fair the arguments seem, though, Ryker is visually presented as the ultimate villain, and this view outweighs anything that he might say to justify his actions.

There are also other changes in the film that disturb the careful reader of the novel. For example, Chris' insults to Shane are much more drastic and too overt, and Shane is seen in the movie as a coward because no man would take such blatant insults and then peacefully leave. One thinks that perhaps Shane really is frightened.

In addition, in the novel, Ernie Wright is goaded by Wilson into drawing; in the movie, young Torrey defies both Ryker and Wilson, almost demanding them to shoot him. Also, in the novel, Shane returns to confront Chris after Chris has spread word around the country that Shane is a coward, and the fight becomes a part of the larger fight, with Ryker (who replaces Morgan as the villain) and his men holding Shane while Ryker viciously beats Shane.

There is one more major difference between the novel and the movie: in the movie, Joe enters the fracas carrying something like a baseball bat, and the viewer is temporarily confused as to whether Joe's violence is the result of his hatred of Ryker, the perennial enemy, or whether it is a result of his coming to Shane's aid.

After the big gunfight, the novel has two more chapters which investigate the effect of the gunfight, but the movie is more dramatically appealing in that, as Shane leaves, the movie ends with the melodramatic and plaintive cries of the young boy calling, "Shane . . . Shane . . . Shane."

Finally, the most significant difference between the novel

and the movie lies in the point of view. The novel emphasized Shane's effect on the young boy – the growing up of a youth in an uncivilized area and the role models whom he has to evaluate life by. The novel is presented from the perspective of the young boy's later life. The movie does not enter into the mind of the boy; we see him only as the worshipper of his super-hero, Shane.

Despite their differences, however, both the movie and the novel have had a tremendous effect on the manner in which we measure the excellence of a western, and both have become classics in their own way.

Western Regional Literature

Any work is defined as "regional" primarily because it takes place in the geographical area known as the West, the South, the Great Plains, or New England. Thus, the western novel is one which takes place in the geographical area known as the West. Accordingly, the setting and the action of the novel are determined by the landscape, climate, and basic geographic features. We will not find swamps or ocean beaches; instead, we will have mountains, valleys, gulches, rock-walled canyons, desolate plains, frontier towns, and vast open spaces.

Of primary concern, therefore, to anyone seeking to discover whether a work of literature is a western regional work is the author's treatment of the land. This is also true of works dealing with the South, for example, and it is certainly true in works dealing with a frontier region, such as the American West. That is, in terms of *Shane*, the basic question is whether or not the land is to be retained as open range for running huge herds of cattle, or whether it is to be parceled out and developed into settled farmland as the homesteaders are attempting to do. Likewise, until the geography of the place has been controlled (whether it be the clearing of the wilderness, as in much southern literature, or controlling the water supply, as in many western works, or as in *Shane*, simply the removal of stumps which interfere with farming), other concerns remain secondary. For example, consider the little town in Willa Cather's

O Pioneers! (1913) as it (the town) tries not to be blown away. Until the town is secure against being blown away, that will continue to be its primary worry.

A fidelity to the facts of geography is required, but it is not to be slavishly adhered to. An author should not go so far as to put in coastlines in the midst of an arid region, or as in a recent TV western show, have the outlaws hiding out in the mountains of Fargo, North Dakota, when in reality the closest mountains to Fargo are the Rocky Mountains, about eight hundred miles away. But, as with the works of Walter Van Tilburg Clark, for the sake of the story in *The Ox-Bow Incident,* he "moves some mountains" across the border to make them be in Nevada.

For the western novel, the land must not only be treated authentically, but it must also be important to the action of the book. In *Shane,* as noted, the ranchers need the open range; the homesteaders need the fences. Also within a region, weather should not be passed over without some comment. The importance of weather in defining a work of western literature lies principally in the rainfall and the ability of the settlers to utilize the natural waters of streams and small rivers. The argument of the ranchers in *Shane* is that the limited water supply is being destroyed by the homesteaders and is being made inaccessible to the herds of cattle belonging to the ranchers. This, of course, is a serious conflict.

Language is also important in determining the regional work. The authors of westerns carefully choose words and idioms which the reading public associates with western speech – words and phrases such as "straight and tall in the saddle," gunslinger, buckaroo, "fast on the draw," rustlers, posse and many more; these words occur continually in western novels.

Likewise, there are certain standard props to be found in typical western literature. The complete list would be enormous, but it would certainly include a horse and a cowboy, or cowhand, or ranchhand, cattle, a large ranch, a small homestead, a "hell-for-leather, smoking six-gun"; a saloon with its bar, whiskey, poker chips and tobacco smoke; fistfights (usually in the barroom, with tables and chairs being broken); a gunslinger and a shootout; rustlers and a posse; trails of stampeding cattle; a picturesque canyon where outlaws could easily hang out; the hero in light-colored clothes and the villain in dark-colored clothes; often, Indians; a stagecoach; lynchings or hangings; ropes and lassos, the stagecoach, hitching posts, a blacksmith and sagebrush; a sheriff and the dance hall girls; and always the wide-open spaces.

Finally, western literature is perhaps most clearly defined by its use of the frontier and new beginnings. The forces of law and order are always combating outlaws in order to bring civilization forward, and the central fact of the western experience is the steady advancement of the frontier line. This line, separating civilization from the wilderness frontier, was a place from which a man could always begin anew, a place where he could shed the entanglements of the past (as apparently Shane is trying to do) and begin an existence which would be free from all past involvements.

Shane and Western Fiction

Sometime around the Civil War era, cheap novels printed on coarse wood pulp paper began to appear; they were loosely and cheaply bound, and after one reading the book probably had to be tossed away. These were often called "dime novels" because they could be purchased for ten cents.

While these novels originally dealt with history, romance, or warfare, one of the most popular types was the western novel. These "dime westerns" attained great popularity partly because of their simplicity of plot, the absence of complex characters, the overt use of conventional moral patterns, the emphasis throughout on nationalistic or patriotic attitudes, and a major emphasis on (1) the strong, individualistic cowboy as hero and (2) the delicate, innocent, helpless female as heroine. These dime westerns were produced by hack writers who emphasized melodrama; any kind of originality was discouraged. All of the heroines were perfect young virgins, and all of the cowboys were god-like representations of perfection. Interestingly, the dime novel of the nineteenth and early twentieth century has re-emerged recently as Harlequin romances – "bodice busters" which crowd our newsstands and which, like the dime novels, offer predigested daydreams to people who cannot dream for themselves.

ZANE GREY   As the dime novel began to disappear, Zane Grey emerged. He wrote more than 55 western novels under his own name and their sales totaled over 13 million copies. He became the twentieth century's foremost writer in the western genre. His works were immensely popular, and his novels usually dealt with a cowboy whose life was always depicted in its most favorable and romantic way. In fact, the romanticizing of the life of the American cowboy and the American West can be largely attributed to the dime novel and to Zane Grey, both contributing heavily to the view of the cowboy found in western movies. Zane Grey's most popular novel was *Riders of the Purple Sage* (1912), but all of his novels were widely read, and many of them have, in part or in total, been used as situational plots for Hollywood movies. Like the dime novels, Grey's stories are usually melodramatic, showing basic conflicts as Schaefer does in *Shane,* but on a more simplistic level: that is, in Grey's works, there is a lack of characterization, and the conflict is most often between a fearless, he-man hero and a ruthless villain with no redeeming qualities; Grey's heroes are self-reliant, brave, and brawny (note, in contrast, how Shane is a modification of this formula – that is, Shane has a dark past, he is slender, and he has more depth of character than do the cowboys of Grey's novels). Throughout his novels, Grey touched on most of the themes and ideas found in today's western novels.

THE LITERARY WESTERN   Walter Van Tilburg Clark's famous novel, *The Ox-Bow Incident,* and Larry McMurtry's

Horseman, Pass By are novels that transcend the typical western novel, yet both works possess most (or many) of the qualities of the typical western novel. Both have also been made into successful movies; the movie of Clark's novel has the same name, but the movie based on McMurtry's novel was renamed *Hud.*

Unlike *Shane*'s opening sentence, the opening sentence of *The Ox-Bow Incident,* "Gil and I crossed the eastern divide about two by the sun," lets us know that this cowboy story is going to be about *two* men rather than about a lonely hero (Shane), but nevertheless, the two opening sentences are similar in that the cowboys ride in from a range far off in the distance.

Ox-Bow is clearly a western novel because it is concerned with such western matters as (1) the western setting, (2) the use of cowboys as narrators and central characters, (3) cattle rustlers, (4) the formation of a posse, (5) the tracking down of outlaws, and (6) the hanging of the captured rustlers. This simplified plot would be enough for a dime novel, a Zane Grey or a Louis L'Amour novel, but Clark adds many dimensions to his novel by, first, making the narrator (one of the cowboys) and his sidekick suspects in the rustling. Also, unlike the traditional western, there are many discussions concerning the nature of justice and injustice, whether or not the captured outlaws should be immediately lynched or tried by a court of law, and then, after the outlaws are lynched and later discovered to be innocent men, there are extended discussions on the nature of a man's guilt for having been involved in the murder of three innocent men. Furthermore, each character is an individual and not a stereotype. Thus, by using these techniques plus an engrossing literary style, Clark takes the typical western novel and elevates it into an in-depth study of mob justice or, more correctly, mob injustice.

Likewise, McMurtry in *Horseman, Pass By* (the successful movie *Hud* stars Paul Newman and Patricia Neal) is able to take a western situation and elevate it to literary merit. The setting is a Texas ranch, and like *Shane,* the movie is narrated from the viewpoint of a young boy who is now in his adulthood, allowing the narrator, like Bob Starrett, to reflect on the significance of the events that took place on his grandfather's ranch.

The central episode of this novel concerns the discovery that one of the boy's grandfather's heifers is found dead of the dreaded hoof and mouth disease. As a result, all of his grandfather's cattle must be destroyed to prevent the spread of the disease. The most powerful scenes in the novel concern the mass slaughter of these cattle. Clearly, McMurtry's novel is elevated to literary status by its investigations into the many individual reactions to this massive slaughter, to this terrible disaster – one that can always befall a cattleman. Thus, as with Clark and Schaefer, it is not merely the plot, but the investigations into the reactions of the characters to any given event that make these novels superior works of literature.

LOUIS L'AMOUR   Today's inheritor of the dime novel mantle and the direct literary descendant of Zane Grey is the contemporary western writer, Louis L'Amour, who has at last count written at least seventy-five western novels; in fact, a new novel appears so frequently that it is difficult to make an exact, or accurate count. Throughout L'Amour's many novels, most of them set in the West from the time of the earliest settlements (as in *The Tall Stranger*), we follow the plight of the first wagon train into the unsettled West to the most modern times (as in *The Gun Slinger*, which takes place in the 1980s). But even in L'Amour's contemporary novels, the setting is still in the West, and the hero is trapped in traditional western situations. For example, in *The Gun Slinger*, the narrator is trapped in a deep canyon ravine, whose rock walls ascend straight up, with no avenue of escape. Meanwhile, other cowboys, on horses, are trying to kill him.

Perhaps L'Amour's major contribution to the western novel lies in the approximately fifteen-plus novels chronicling the fates and fortunes of the Sackett family, especially Jubal Sackett. In writing about this family, L'Amour has created a panoramic and historic view of one dominant family over a long period of time and has used this family in order to present a brief history of the settlement of the West.

For the most part, L'Amour's other novels resort to using one-dimensional characters with simple motives. The appeal is most often focused on simple narrative action. These novels are usually filled with minor inconsistencies which would not bother the average reader, but which would probably disturb the more discriminating critic of literature. Ultimately, however, it is L'Amour's use of the simple, old-fashioned macho type hero and the lovely, often helpless heroine which has the most permanent appeal to the modern reader.

In general, the western novel – both in its cheapest form and in its most elevated literary rendition – has continued to appeal to the reading public since its first appearance in the nineteenth century, and at present, it seems that it will continue to appeal to the modern reader for some time in the future.

Shane and the Classical Plot

As noted elsewhere in these Notes, Schaefer studied classical Greek literature at Columbia University. Later on in his life, in an interview, he said of his writings that he wanted primarily to be a good storyteller, meaning perhaps in the sense that the ancient Greek writers were some of the Western world's best storytellers. The key emphasis in Greek literature was upon the narrative plot, or the simple storyline. Aristotle, the first critic of literature, emphasized that of all the elements of literature, the plot was the most important, and then came character and setting, language, scenery and so forth. Certainly, Schaefer's main concern in *Shane* is with the plot; it is an absorbing story which holds the readers of all ages in suspense. Then, too, Schaefer is interested in character, especially the character of Shane. (And as it was with the ancient Greeks, Schaefer's main character here has only one name.) After plot and character, Schaefer makes good use of his western setting.

The point is this: there are only so many ways of telling a good story, and it seems that Schaefer hit upon one that goes back to classical antiquity. It is a tried and tested archetypal plot. In its most simplified and extended patterns, *Shane* follows the classical pattern that was set in around 420 B.C., during the classical age of Greek literature. Note the following parallels in outline form between the action, or plot, of the classical Greek play *Oedipus* and the novel *Shane*.

Oedipus arrives in Thebes.	Shane arrives in the valley.
Oedipus is unknown.	Shane is unknown.
There is a time of prosperity.	There is a time of prosperity.
There is a plague upon the land.	Fletcher is a plague upon the land.
Oedipus solves the plague.	Shane solves the problems of the valley.
After the plague is solved, Oedipus leaves.	After the problems are solved, Shane rides away.

SUGGESTED ESSAY QUESTIONS

1. Write an essay on the basic appeal of the lonely cowboy who comes from nowhere and disappears into the unknown.

2. What is the nature of the conflict between the rancher (or cattle baron) and the homesteaders? Write a description of this conflict so that each side appears to have sound arguments.

3. How is our view of Shane affected by our being limited to knowing only the things that the young Bob Starrett is able to comprehend?

4. Describe the differences between Shane and Joe Starrett, both in their physical statures and in what each of them stands for, or believes in.

5. In spite of Shane's unknown background, he becomes a legend in the valley. How is he idealized – not only by young Bob, but by the rest of the community?

SELECTED BIBLIOGRAPHY

CAWELTI, JOHN G. *The Six-Gun Mystique.* Bowling Green: Bowling Green State University Popular Press, 1970.

CLEARY, MICHAEL. "Jack Schaefer: The Evolution of Pessimism." *Western American Literature* 14 (May, 1979), 33–47.

ERISMAN, FRED. "Growing Up with the American West: Fiction of Jack Schaefer." *Popular Press:* Bowling Green State University, 1974.

FOLSOM, JAMES K. "*Shane* and Hud: Two Stories in Search of a Medium." *Western Humanities Review* 24, no. 4 (Autumn, 1970), 359–72.

HASLAM, GERALD. *Jack Schaefer.* Boise State University Western Writers Series, no. 20 (1975).

MARSDEN, MICHAEL T. "Savior in the Saddle: The Sagebrush Testament," *Focus on the Western.* Englewood Cliffs, N.J.: Prentice-Hall, 1974.

_____. "*Shane:* From Magazine Serial to American Classic." *South Dakota Review* 15, no. 4 (Winter, 1977–78), 59–67.

MIKKELSEN, ROBERT. "The Western Writer: Jack Schaefer's Use of the Western Frontier," *Western Humanities Review* 8, no. 2 (Spring, 1954).

NOTES

NOTES

NOTES

NOTES

NOTES

NOTES